VANCOUVER

VANCOUVER

EXPLORER
OF THE PACIFIC COAST

RONALD SYME

illustrated by WILLIAM STOBBS

William Morrow and Company New York

The English fishermen sluicing down the holds of their herring boats in the North Sea port of King's Lynn knew George Vancouver when he was a small boy. Almost every day he walked solemnly out along the stone quay to the lighthouse at its end. The men came to recognize his familiar figure in flat-crowned, stiff-brimmed hat, stout blue jacket, and black shoes with bright, square buckles.

The sailors were amused by the way George

plodded along in his serious fashion, mittened hands clasped behind his back, a solemn expression on his face. The cold and blustering wind off the sea often turned his cheeks a glowing red. But the fishermen were impressed by George's precocious knowledge of all the different types of vessels that came landward to find shelter in the harbor.

Every now and then they liked to test that knowledge with questions. His answers always made the fishermen grin and nod approvingly. Not often, they said, did an eleven-year-old boy know, as George did, that a barquentine was square-rigged on the foremast only. On a barque, he would tell them, *all* the masts carried square sails except the one nearest the stern.

In the 1760's, the port of King's Lynn on the east coast of England was an excellent place in which to study many different types of vessels. The North Sea, stretching between the western coast of Europe and the eastern shores of England, was already one of the great ocean highways of the world. Northward along it to Iceland and Newfoundland went the fishing fleets of different countries; southward came the great Baltic freighters with their cargoes of pitch and timber, ropes and barrels of salt fish. Sometimes a black-hulled British warship with the line of her gunports painted bright yellow came cruising along in majestic manner. Lean, fast-sailing Spanish merchantmen, high-decked at bow and stern, also glided into King's Lynn to land cargoes of silk and wine, hides and copper and cork. When they sailed, they carried away good English wool, iron machinery, and textiles.

George knew all the ships. He also knew the cargoes they handled, and if he ever was in doubt he merely had to ask his father. John Vancouver was the Collector of Customs at King's Lynn. His position was an important, well-paid, and responsible one. But a commercial occupation of any kind was regarded in those days as unworthy of a gentleman, so John Vancouver had proved his respectability by marrying Bridget Berners. She was the daughter of a wealthy land-owning squire, whose country estate lay within a few miles of King's Lynn.

Young George Vancouver was like his Dutch and English forebears. Sturdy, honest, and rather unimaginative people, over the years they had diligently minded their own business, been a trifle close-fisted with money, and kept out of rowdy local politics. George's mother was displeased by her son's love of the sea, and she and her father tried to interest him in the virtues of country life.

Squire Berners and Bridget Vancouver might have succeeded in influencing George had it not been for a great event that took place in July, 1771, when George was fourteen

8

years old. At that time Captain James Cook returned to England from his first great voyage of discovery in the little known South Pacific Ocean. The British government was already planning a second voyage for him. Captain Cook was to search for the mysterious continent that was supposed to lie far to the south in the unexplored seas between New Zealand and South Africa.

In his younger days, Cook had been employed as an officer on coal-carrying vessels owned by the Walker brothers that plied up and down the North Sea. Mr. Vancouver remembered him as being very punctual and diligent and a fine navigator. Now George became fascinated by everything about Cook's recent around-the-world voyage. He found a couple of seamen who had sailed with Cook in the 500-ton collier, *Freelove*. From these veterans he gained more knowledge of the great explorer.

"I want to sail with Captain Cook on his next voyage," he suddenly informed his parents. "Perhaps the Walkers will speak to him on my behalf."

Once George expressed an intention, he seldom discussed it again or changed his mind at a later date. Although his mother pleaded with him not to act hastily, he persuaded his father to write to the Walkers and ask for a letter of introduction to the famous Captain Cook.

Vancouver received an immediate and favorable response from Cook. As a result, in June, 1772, when he was fifteen years old, George Vancouver helped carry his brass-bound sea chest aboard Captain Cook's new ship, the *Resolution.*

The vessel was a former coal carrier that the Navy had bought from her previous owners. Being heavily built and having enormous storage space, Cook believed that the ship was

ideal for long voyages and had a good chance of surviving the toughest usage.

According to Naval custom in those days, a boy who wanted to become a seagoing officer spent six years at sea in training. First he served at least a year or two as a Volunteer, or, as it was more commonly known, a King's Letter Boy, referring to the fact that the boy was marked as a future midshipman and officer. The life of a Volunteer in the 1700's was the toughest existence a reasonably well educated boy could choose for himself. The experience either made or broke him. If he survived shipwreck, scurvy, Naval battles, appalling food, and long service in bad climates, he could become a highly trained lieutenant on a wage of less than a dollar a day. It was not surprising that many Volunteers failed to complete the course and become officers.

Aboard the *Resolution,* the young gentlemen,

as they also sometimes were known, lived in a damp, low, and stuffy compartment near the stern of the ship. It was below the waterline and smelled of stale cheese, moldy clothes, and human bodies. The only furniture consisted of a table and a cutlass rack. The boys used their sea chests as chairs and slept in hammocks. While in their own quarters they were under the discipline of the commissioned gunner. Every morning, except Sundays, they attended classes in navigation, trigonometry, and elementary science run on board by a schoolmaster. At certain set times the boys acted as general assistants to the officer in charge of the deck watch. For any breach of discipline, they were harshly beaten with a leather-bound cane.

Volunteer Vancouver was short, somewhat plump, round faced, and a trifle slow on his feet. He seldom smiled, spoke little, but—as the officers soon noticed—he obeyed orders in

a careful and deliberate manner. Captain Cook chose only the most efficient seamen for his crew, and he had taken on Vancouver because Lieutenant Cooper, his second-in-command, had been well impressed by him.

In July, 1772, Vancouver sailed on one of the most interesting voyages in the history of exploration. Apart from its fascinating destination, this voyage also became remarkable for the way in which Captain Cook kept his

men free of the dreaded illness called scurvy. The seamen detested and gumbled at the strange dishes he made sure were included in their daily diet. They only wanted salt pork, beef, and dried peas—their usual fare. However, Cook provided them with extras in the form of pickled cabbage, malt, a peculiar-tasting beer, and something officially described as carrot marmalade. They either ate these foods or were given the lash.

But however much they muttered and brooded among themselves, resented scrubbing out their accommodations with vinegar, and airing their blankets on deck, the sailors knew that Cook's unpopular methods worked. They would stay alive and healthy when, in almost any other vessel afloat, perhaps half of them would be dead inside two years at sea.

Around South Africa sailed the little *Resolution* and her even smaller companion, the *Adventure.* They went down into the bitter, icy seas of the high latitudes near the Antarctic Circle, thence onward to a safe harbor in the South Island of New Zealand, a country inhabited at that time by the tough, warlike, unpredictable yet oddly likeable Maori race. On June 3, 1773, which happened to be a few days before Vancouver's sixteenth birthday, Cook wrote:

Yesterday morning a man brought his son, a

boy of about ten years of age, and presented him to me. . . . I thought he wanted to sell him, but at last found out that he wanted me to give him a shirt, which I accordingly did. The boy was so fond of his new dress that he went all over the ship, presenting himself to everybody who came in his way.

George Vancouver, instead of pacing the chilly quay of King's Lynn, now frequently strolled along the silent and beautiful shore of Queen Charlotte's Sound, in the Solomon Islands, curiously observed by the local tattooed cannibals. In August that same year, the ships lay anchored off the shores of the high and wonderfully beautiful island of Tahiti. In October, Vancouver and the other Volunteers were exploring the picturesque lanes that wound across the lovely countryside of Tonga, a group of islands a thousand miles to the southwest of Tahiti.

Three months later, in January, 1774, the

17

Resolution was alone in the Antarctic, having accidentally lost contact with the *Adventure.* On the thirtieth of that month, when Cook had ventured well inside the Antarctic Circle, high crags and pinnacles of solid pack ice barred all further progress to his little ship. As it was impossible to maintain their course, Cook gave the order to put about and steer northward.

As the *Resolution* hesitated and began to swing around, Vancouver ran toward the bow in his heavy clothing. Having gone as far forward as he could, he solemnly raised his arm and shouted: *"Ne plus ultra!"* (The utmost point.) He had, in fact, approached nearer to the South Pole—by perhaps half the length of the ship—than any other member of the crew. His claim continued to hold good for many years after, and Vancouver himself was always oddly proud of this distinction.

The remarkable voyage continued. Two months after leaving the Antarctic, the *Resolu-*

tion was again back in the sunlit seas of the South Pacific. Toward the end of July, 1774, Vancouver and the other young gentlemen were cautiously looking at black-skinned and treacherous native warriors in New Guinea from a boat floating within a few yards of the shore. He missed being present, however, on the day that a crowd of these warriors charged another boat from the *Resolution,* firing arrows and hurling poison-tipped spears as they came. The natives were driven back by musket fire from the crew.

"Happily for many of these people," Cook wrote kindly, "not half of our muskets would go off, otherwise many more of them must have fallen."

In October, 1774, the *Resolution* was again in New Zealand. Vancouver and his companions went shooting wildfowl along the coast. They were unaware that the Maori natives who smiled and greeted them with an

affable *"Tena koe"* (good day to you) had recently murdered and eaten one midshipman and ten sailors from the *Adventure*.

In August, 1775, more than three years after his departure, eighteen-year-old George Vancouver came home to his parents' black-and-white timbered house in King's Lynn.

An eager family and numerous friends pleaded for news of his voyage with the greatest navigator alive. But George was a trifle tiresome. He spoke gravely of latitudes and longitudes and liked to describe different climates and unusual coastlines. Only now and then did he interest his slightly bored listeners by letting fall some surprising remark such as: "It was in the New Hebrides that the petty officers fired at the wild fellows who hurled stones at us." Or: "We were greatly alarmed when Captain Cook nearly died after eating a poisonous gourd fish."

If his parents hoped that George's long voyage had cured him of his liking for a life at sea, they were quickly disappointed. He made it clear to them that in spite of the clammy discomfort of the *Resolution's* gunroom and the horrors of carrot marmalade and pickled cabbage, he was very pleased with the way things had turned out. So pleased was he, in fact, that he hoped to accompany Captain Cook on another voyage in the near future.

This proposed voyage was already being discussed by severe gentlemen in wigs sitting around a large polished table in the British Admiralty. They were warmly interested in the ancient theory of a Northwest Passage between Hudson Bay and the Pacific Ocean.

A plucky Canadian trapper named Samuel Hearne had recently explored a vast area of territory to the northwest of Hudson Bay. He had come across no trace of any sea passage in that quarter. Since then Hearne had stated openly his belief that any such passage must lie much farther north than geographers thought. Now the British government was offering a reward worth 100,000 dollars to the first man to locate a passage between the Pacific and the Atlantic Oceans.

Two hundred years before, the Spanish explorer Juan de Fuca announced that he had found some kind of a sea passage far to the north of New Albion (California). And then nearly one hundred and fifty years later the Danish explorer Vitus Bering discovered the strait that runs between America and Asia. Perhaps the long-sought sea passage opened off the southern end of this strait? Its northern end was not suitable owing to ice all the year around. For the past hundred years or so, explorers had been searching for the eastern, or Atlantic, end of the Northwest Passage. They had found nothing. Now the Lords of the Admiralty decided to send an expedition to search for a *western* entrance somewhere at the southern end of Bering Strait.

Cook was invited by the Admiralty to undertake this third voyage of exploration, into arctic waters this time, far from the friendly islands and warm trade winds of the South Pacific.

"The captain writes that I may join his expedition," George informed his family one morning after receiving a letter from Cook.

"The *Resolution* will be sailing again, but not the *Adventure*. She's to be replaced by another smaller collier called the *Discovery*."

After more study of the letter George added further news. "I am to sail in the *Discovery* under Captain Clerke, who worked his way up from able seaman under Captain Cook. The captain declares that I am to receive an appointment as midshipman."

In January, 1778, Vancouver took part in the discovery of the more westerly Hawaiian Islands. In June he was above the Arctic Circle in the freezing waters of the Bering Strait. Cook was carrying out his orders to "search for and to explore such rivers or inlets as may appear to be of considerable extent, and pointing towards Hudson's or Baffin's Bay." The northern limit he reached was closed by ice almost all the year.

When the end of the northern summer made further exploration impossible, the two ships sailed southward to the Hawaiian Islands to take on fresh provisions, overhaul the ships, and refresh the crews. In November of that same year of 1778, Vancouver was one of the first to take a compass bearing on a headland of the newly discovered island of Hawaii. They finally anchored in Kealakekua Bay on the westerly coast of that island.

The handsome, brown-skinned Hawaiian people at first believed that these visitors were the great white gods of their legends and traditions. The diary of a member of the group related the reaction of the natives, who said:

> The men are white. Their skin is loose [meaning their clothes]. Their heads are three-cornered [a reference to the shape of the hats of that period]. They have long hair like women [pigtails were then fashionable]. They are volcanoes, for fire and smoke issue from their mouths [tobacco pipes]. They have doors in the side of their bodies [pockets]. Their bodies are full of treasure.

The Hawaiians were soon disillusioned. The rough and forthright seamen of the eighteenth century were certainly not even remotely connected with the gods of Polynesia. When the sailors' voracious appetites caused a shortage of food in Hawaii, friendship between the two races rapidly faded. Hostile incidents began to occur. A native on board the *Discovery* snatched some tools from the deck and leaped over the side into his canoe. Edgar, one of the junior officers, and Vancouver went off in pursuit with a boatload of men.

The thief had fled by the time the boat reached the shore. Edgar managed to get back the stolen tools and decided to confiscate the canoe used by the thief. A number of Hawaiians objected. A scuffle began, and a seaman knocked down one of the natives. Another Hawaiian picked up the broken shaft of an oar and swung a blow at Edgar. Edgar wrote later:

The man most certainly would have knocked me off the rock [on which he was standing] into the water, if Mr. Vancouver, the Midshipman, had not at this instant stepped out of the pinnace between the Indian [Hawaiian] and me, and received the blow, which took him on the side and knocked him down.

Edgar hurried off to make his report to Captain Cook, who was also on the beach, but some distance away. Poor Vancouver and his nine or ten sailors were left to confront a crowd of brawny, angry, and threatening Hawaiians.

The fight began almost at once.

The Hawaiians made a rush at the boat with the intention of stripping off all its iron and brass fittings. A burly Hawaiian picked up Vancouver and threw him to the ground. As he jumped up, the seamen came to his assistance. The fight swirled and eddied around the boat for several minutes. At length a friendly young chieftain arrived and put an end to it. The seamen picked up Vancouver, who had been knocked down several more times, and dusted him off. They were unable, however, to locate his hat, which had gotten lost in the struggle. Even then the British seamen, including Cook himself, made the tragic mistake of underestimating the increasing resentment of the Hawaiian people.

At daybreak the following morning, February 14, the crew of the *Discovery* reported that one of their boats had been stolen during the night. The line attaching it to the ship's side had been deliberately cut. This theft was the last straw as far as Cook was concerned. He informed Lieutenant King that they must seize a Hawaiian hostage at once and keep him aboard the *Resolution* until the boat was returned. Cook then loaded a double-barreled shotgun with bird shot in one chamber and solid lead ball in the other. Accompanied by an armed party of nine marines under Lieu-

32

tenant Phillips, he was rowed ashore in one of the two boats that left the ship.

Cook, still in a furious mood, landed on the beach and walked fifty yards ashore to the thatched cottage of King Kalaniopu. Arousing that sleepy monarch from his mat, Cook attempted to lead him to the doorway and down to the boat. But several hundred hostile Hawaiians began running toward the cottage. Cook, realizing he could not take the king without causing bloodshed, let Kalaniopu go.

Cook began walking back to the boats. Suddenly an angry warrior darted at him with a leveled spear. Cook raised his shotgun and fired at the man, mercifully using the barrel containing bird shot. This light charge failed to penetrate the warrior's shield. He came on again. Cook then fired the second barrel, killing a man standing directly behind the warrior. A moment later the nine marines, lined up at the water's edge, fired an uneven volley

and began retreating to the boats. Cook turned to give a command to the marines—probably to tell them to cease firing—when he was stabbed in the back and fell with his face in the water. On seeing him fall, the islanders set up a great shout and dragged his body onto the shore.

The early-morning fight lasted only ten minutes. At the end of it Captain Cook and four marines lay dead on the beach. The boats

with their wounded and badly shaken crews hastily returned to the ships. That night the Hawaiians burned the captain's corpse on a funeral pyre high on the hills overlooking Kealakekua Bay.

By February 21, tempers had cooled and two high-born Hawaiians came aboard the *Resolution* and brought with them the remaining bones of Captain Cook, part of his gun, his shoes, and some other relics. These remains were committed to the deep blue waters of the bay with a full ceremony of naval honors.

Such was the passing of Captain Cook, who charted the Pacific Ocean with incomparable accuracy and, while he was doing that, also demonstrated how to avoid scurvy.

Once more the ships left the subtropical latitudes of the Pacific, and after a dispirited further search for the Northwest Passage in Bering Strait both ships returned to England in October, 1780. Arctic ice conditions were extremely bad that year.

On this last voyage Vancouver had been away from home for four years and three months. Early in 1781 he successfully passed his examination for a lieutenancy. In October of that same year, Cornwallis surrendered at Yorktown and the American Revolution came to an end.

But Britain still remained at war with France and Spain. Accordingly, the Navy had plenty of work to do. Down in the stormy West Indies in 1782, Lieutenant Vancouver, in the little sloop of war *Martin,* commanded by Captain Merrick, signaled to a suspect passing vessel to heave to. The captain answered he came from Cartagena bound to Havana. Captain Merrick then asked him to shorten sail immediately. He answered that he would, but instead he fired a broadside at the *Martin,* which she immediately answered, and both ships kept continually firing for nearly two hours.

Approaching darkness put a temporary end to the fight. Throughout a hot and windless night both ships remained floating idly within range of each other. As daylight returned they began firing again. The Spanish ship—for such it turned out to be—surrendered soon after sunrise.

Vancouver remained in the West Indies until 1783 when a peace treaty was signed in

Europe. He spent a year patrolling dangerous channels and bays, visiting primitive tropical islands, running for shelter before the menace of approaching hurricanes, and watching his companions die of the dreaded yellow fever.

Twenty-six-year-old Vancouver remained unaffected by all this extra experience. Eleven years older now than when he had joined the *Resolution* as a King's Letter Boy, he still carried out orders in a deliberate manner, seldom displayed any emotion, and kept his thoughts to himself. But in his eight-by-four-foot cabin he carefully wrote notes on his unceasing struggle to discover the means of eliminating scurvy not only from his own vessel but throughout the entire British Navy. On a tiny shelf above his bunk were all the best and latest textbooks on navigation. Senior Naval officers on the West Indies station were beginning to regard Lieutenant Vancouver as a most competent young officer. They noted approvingly that he neither drank nor gambled and that his professional duties always came first.

The Navy rewarded him inconsiderately. In July, 1783, Vancouver was back in King's Lynn, a temporarily unemployed officer on half pay.

"There are thousands of young officers in the same condition as yourself." said shrewd old John Vancouver. "Should you choose to resign your commission, I will use my interest to find attractive employment for you on land. Living on half pay will not make you plump in the pockets."

George still refused to abandon his seafaring life. For eighteen months he made unceasing efforts to secure another ship, and in November, 1784 he succeeded. Back he went to the West Indies on a small and rather insignificant Naval vessel.

Peace now had returned to Europe. The Navy's only task was to cruise leisurely around Caribbean waters, keeping on the alert for pirates. Vancouver passed his spare time in making minor corrections to his charts and trying to convince thick-headed Navy officials that it was cheaper and more humane to feed sailors on a proper diet instead of allowing many of them to die of scurvy every year.

In 1786, about a year after Vancouver returned to Jamaica, Commodore Sir Alan Gardner arrived to take command of the West

Indies squadron. This grim old veteran had been brought up in the traditional Navy style, but in some way he had managed to preserve a fresh and original mind. He discovered very quickly that scurvy was a serious problem in the ships under his command. He also found out that Vancouver was the only officer who had tried to introduce local fruit and vegetables aboard the vessels. Gardner sent for Vancouver to discuss the matter.

"I want you to let me have a list of all citrus and other fruits that we can obtain in Jamaica," said Gardner. "When I have it, I'll tolerate no delay or opposition on the matter of proper diet for the men."

Lemons, limes, oranges, and mangoes appeared aboard the ships. The health of the sailors rapidly improved and the death rate declined. Commodore Gardner, who seldom went out of his way to show benevolence to junior officers, made Vancouver an exception.

Some time later the commodore received instructions from the Admiralty to arrange for accurate charts to be prepared of all bays and harbors in Jamaica. On making inquiries as to which officer was best qualified to undertake this work, Vancouver's name was again mentioned.

"A very promising young officer," Gardner muttered approvingly. "Tell him to report to me."

To Vancouver himself, Gardner said, "You were fortunate to learn survey work under Captain Cook. He was the finest—quite the finest—navigator the Navy's ever produced. You will undertake the charting of the Jamaica coast, Mr. Vancouver. Choose whom you wish as your assistant."

Vancouver picked to assist him a senior non-commissioned officer named Joseph Whidbey. In those days many senior Naval officers were somewhat limited in their understanding of advanced navigation. The Naval authorities found it wiser to have on board all vessels a sailing master, who was expert in navigation and also had a vast amount of knowledge about the ship in other respects as well. The master ranked lower than the lieutenants but above the warrant officers, and was a very respected and responsible member of the crew.

Whidbey was the sailing master of the *Europa,* Vancouver's own ship. He was a short, burly, brown-faced veteran with a terse and capable manner, and an enormous amount of knowledge about everything connected with ships and the sea. Vancouver and he made a laconic and efficient pair.

They spent long hours every day in a ship's boat, noting depths and checking compass bearings. It was hot, tiresome, and monotonous work in the blistering West Indian climate, where spells of tropical sunshine alternated with torrential showers. But when Commodore Gardner saw the first of the finished charts Vancouver submitted to him, he nodded approvingly.

Gardner returned to England in 1789. Later in that same year Vancouver followed him. He was promoted to first lieutenant, and then placed once again on half pay and left with little choice but to return to his home in King's Lynn. Commodore Gardner, however, was appointed to a high position in the Admiralty.

In the same year of 1789 a famous international uproar began over a primitive and insignificant little inlet named Nootka Sound off the Pacific coast. To Vancouver the bay was King George's Sound, the name given to it by Cook in 1778.

The Spanish administration of Peru had sent men and ships northward to found the white-walled little settlement of San Francisco in 1775. A year or so later their explorers had discovered Nootka Sound. Its gloomy surrounding hills and dark pine forests did not appeal to the sun-loving Spaniards. They thought nothing more of the place until a number of British trading vessels, some of them commanded by officers who had sailed along this coast with Captain Cook, began to use Nootka Sound as a handy base for trading in sea-otter pelts with China. In return for the furs, they obtained enormous quantities of tea.

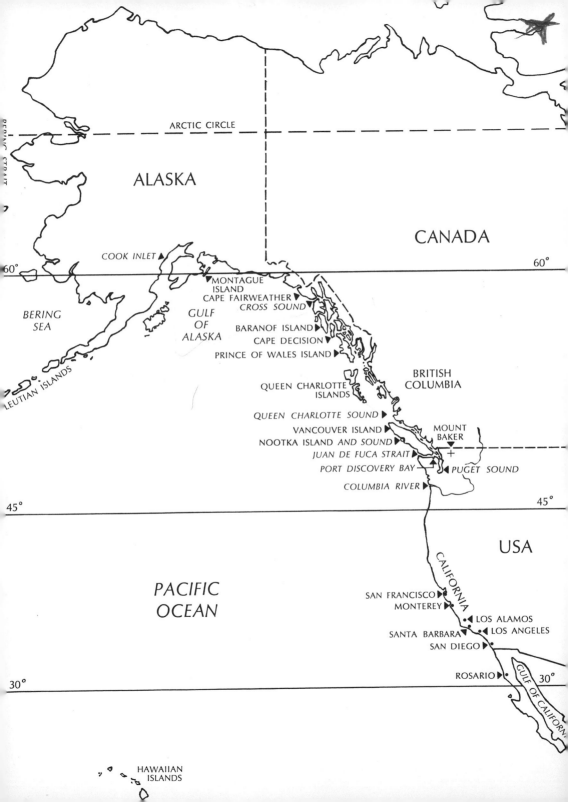

ARCTIC CIRCLE

ALASKA

CANADA

COOK INLET ▶

60°   60°

MONTAGUE
ISLAND
CAPE FAIRWEATHER ▶
CROSS SOUND ▶

BERING
SEA

GULF
OF
ALASKA

BARANOF ISLAND ▶
CAPE DECISION ▶
PRINCE OF WALES ISLAND ▶

BRITISH
COLUMBIA

LEUTIAN ISLANDS

QUEEN CHARLOTTE
ISLANDS

QUEEN CHARLOTTE SOUND ▶
VANCOUVER ISLAND ▶   MOUNT
NOOTKA ISLAND AND SOUND ▶   BAKER
JUAN DE FUCA STRAIT ▶   +
PORT DISCOVERY BAY ◀   ◀ PUGET SOUND
COLUMBIA RIVER ▶

45°   45°

USA

PACIFIC
OCEAN

CALIFORNIA

SAN FRANCISCO ▶
MONTEREY ▶
                              ◀ LOS ALAMOS
SANTA BARBARA ▶   ◀ LOS ANGELES
SAN DIEGO ▶

ROSARIO ▶   30°   GULF OF CALIFORNIA
30°

HAWAIIAN
ISLANDS

The Spanish promptly objected. They pointed out that between 1774 and 1788 their own ships had sailed as far north as the Gulf of Alaska. They regarded the entire Pacific coast as their own territory. A couple of Spanish warships arrived in Nootka Sound, and British traders who had begun to erect small wooden storage sheds between the beach and the forest were ordered to quit.

England promptly pointed out that one of her captains, Sir Francis Drake, had reached the California coast in 1579. After anchoring in the "faire and good Baye" of San Francisco, he had named the country Nova Albion and set up a monument to mark the English monarch's right and title to the place.

In other words, England had beaten Spain to the California coast by about 200 years. She believed that her ships had, if anything, more right to use Nootka Sound than those of Spain.

England was rich, powerful, and obstinate.

Spain was proud and temperamental. Neither side would yield to the other. Both began to look for allies. England secured Holland; Spain was secretly negotiating with France.

When both countries were on the verge of war, Spain suddenly gave way. France was in a revolutionary state and not to be depended on. England was informed that Spain was prepared to hand over Nootka Sound and to compensate the evicted traders.

The Admiralty decided to send a vessel to Nootka in order to settle final details with the Spanish representatives on the spot. At the same time this ship would make a proper survey of the Pacific coast and carry on the search begun by Cook for a Northwest Passage—a responsible mission for some officer.

"Vancouver's the man," said Admiral (formerly Commodore) Gardner. "A first-class navigator and his survey work is very expert. He was off the Pacific coast with Cook and knows what conditions are like up there. Give him a couple of ships, and he'll survey as much coast as we wish. Aye, and he'll come back with his men in good health too."

Vancouver was recalled from King's Lynn and sent hurrying by coach to the Admiralty. He found that after seventeen years as an obscure Naval officer, he was at last to command his own vessel and undertake an important task.

The *Discovery* was named perhaps after Cook's famous little vessel. She was of only 340 tons, three-masted, and measured 79 feet in length along her keel. Her companion was a two-masted clumsy-looking little store ship named the *Chatham,* of a mere 120 tons. No one liked this little ship except Lieutenant William Broughton, who—like Vancouver— was about to receive his first command.

A number of important civilians were interested in the forthcoming voyage. One of them was Sir Joseph Banks, a brilliant amateur naturalist who had accompanied Cook on his first voyage to the Pacific. Banks wanted a great deal of space aboard the *Discovery* in which to erect a greenhouse for the botanical specimens to be collected by Dr. Archibald Menzies, the naturalist who would accompany the vessel.

Glass greenhouses and ships did not go well together in Vancouver's forthright view. He said so to Sir Joseph in polite but terse words. Being a prominent and influential man, Sir Joseph did not enjoy being thwarted.

"How Vancouver will behave to you is more than I can guess," he wrote to Menzies, "unless I was to judge by his conduct toward me, which was such as I am not accustomed to receive from one of his rank."

The *Discovery,* with 101 men aboard, and the *Chatham,* with 45 men, sailed from England early in April, 1791. The splendidly named Zachary Mudge was Vancouver's first lieutenant. Her three junior lieutenants were Peter

Puget, Joseph Baker, and the recently promoted Joseph Whidbey—now clad in a handsome gold-laced blue coat and white knee breeches with silk stockings. The youngest member of the *Discovery's* crew was Thomas Heddington, a midshipman, aged fifteen.

Under blue skies and with a fine brisk breeze coming up from astern, Vancouver worried about the little Chatham's apparent lack of speed. "Make more sail," he signaled almost daily to her, much to Broughton's annoyance. Yet oddly enough, the *Chatham* reached the Canary Islands off West Africa well before the *Discovery.*

On the way to South Africa, Vancouver —who was showing some irritation and impatience at this early stage of the voyage —signaled *Chatham* that he proposed to go ahead and leave her to catch up with him at Capetown. When Vancouver sailed into that vast and splendid harbor, the *Chatham* was already there, having arrived twenty-four hours earlier. Broughton, with a perfectly serious face, saluted on her poop.

After crossing the Indian Ocean, Vancouver surveyed nearly 400 miles of the little-known coast of South Australia. In November, seven months after leaving England, the two ships entered silent and beautiful Dusky Bay on the coast of the South Island of New Zealand, where Cook had anchored on several occasions.

Nearby was an inlet that Cook, not having the leisure to explore, had humorously named on his chart, "Nobody Knows What." This flippancy did not appeal to Vancouver's serious mind. In a ship's boat he diligently surveyed the inlet and found that it was divided into two channels.

"The heads of these arms I have called, 'Somebody Knows What,'" he solemnly entered in his official record, or log.

The ships sailed onward to Tahiti. Once again Vancouver gloomily eyed the little *Chatham* bouncing and swaying along astern in a tremendous nor'easterly gale. This time she was certain to be left behind. Yet when the *Discovery* reached Matávai (Shining Water) Bay in Tahiti, Lieutenant Broughton was again saluting on the poop. The *Chatham* had managed to arrive three days previously.

Vancouver remained in Tahiti for a month. He knew from earlier experience that whenever sailors went ashore and began to mix freely with the natives, discipline slackened and trouble often arose. He ordered that only those men of known good character should be allowed to land. The rest of the crew were left to lean on the rails and gaze longingly at the picturesque thatched cottages and green hills of the beautiful island.

This iron-hard discipline served its purpose. The Tahitians supplied the ships with all the fresh meat and vegetables required and were delighted with the honest manner in which they received payment in the form of knives and iron nails, which they used to make excellent fishing hooks and chisels. Vancouver, who spoke their language reasonably well, was one of the very few sea captains of those days who treated the islanders with courtesy, consideration, and friendship. He had inherited this attitude of respect from the humane Cook.

At the end of February, 1792, nearly a year after leaving England, the ships reached the Hawaiian Islands.

Now began a difficult time for Vancouver. He liked these handsome islands and admired the Hawaiian people. But he could not forget that thirteen years ago Captain Cook had been struck down on the long white beach of Kealakekua Bay. The rich blue skies and the soothing murmur of the trade wind were unable to tempt him to ignore that tragic event. He remained nervous and suspicious of the Hawaiians. Once he saw a large grass fire on a distant hillside where natives were clearing land before planting sugar cane. "Captain Vancouver thought proper to torture his mind," wrote Midshipman Manby of the *Discovery*, "with ill-founded suspicion. . . . He construed it to be the flaming signal for war."

On another occasion, when the surf was running too high for the ships' boats to land, Vancouver tried to reach the shore in an outrigger canoe manned by a sturdy Hawaiian crew. It was sheer misfortune that the canoe was swamped and that Vancouver and a midshipman were washed overboard. Another canoe hoisted both of them aboard, but not before the midshipman had swallowed a lot of water. Vancouver was convinced that the Hawaiians had tried to drown him. When he wished to return to his ship later that day, he refused to board another canoe but swam out through the surf—a remarkable feat for anyone unaccustomed to those giant seas—to be picked up by one of his own boats.

There was, however, some justification

for Vancouver's constant suspicion. The natives had captured and looted the American brig *Fair Lady* the previous year. They had learned the killing power of firearms and were no longer interested in bartering for nails and knives. They were prepared to go to great lengths to obtain muskets and pistols.

"We have been informed," noted Vancouver in his log, "that these islanders have tried various schemes to destroy the crews and to gain possession of some of the trading vessels."

The *Discovery* and *Chatham* sailed for the American coast on March 16 and sighted New Albion, or California, in the middle of April. They reached the coast about eighty miles north of San Francisco, and at this point Vancouver began his tremendous survey.

His orders were to examine and chart

the coast from a latitude of 30 degrees north, or in a line with the northernmost part of the Gulf of California, to the southern coast of Alaska. "To discover if possible any water communication which may assist intercourse for the purpose of commerce [in simpler language, a passage for merchant ships] between the northwest coast, and the country [Canada] upon the opposite side of the Continent."

No accurate maps existed to guide Vancouver. The only general chart of the coast in his possession was that made during Cook's third voyage. The Spaniards had their own maps—of doubtful accuracy— of the coast, but they had no intention of sharing them with anyone else.

Lieutenant Whidbey, dourly surveying the misty blue coast from the *Discovery,* summed up his feelings with the words: "What with uncertain weather and shoal water and

60

only the summer months to work in, this present commission is the outside of enough."

All that summer of 1792 the ships edged their way up the coast to Nootka Sound, where the Spanish authorities had been notified of their pending arrival. During the daytime the ships sailed at a distance of about two miles from the shore. On the high poop of the *Discovery,* Vancouver and his officers were constantly at work with their instruments. They kept the coast under continual examination with heavy brass telescopes, took compass bearings at frequent intervals, and made numerous sketches of unusual landmarks. The *Chatham,* moving farther inshore, sent away her boats to make a closer investigation of every doubtful bay or other opening. At sunset every evening the ships headed out to sea and lay some ten miles off the coast until sunrise the following morning. They then returned to the point where they had ended their survey the previous day.

And yet, despite his meticulous care, Vancouver missed the entrance to the big Columbia River. He wrote about this area:

The sea changed from its natural, to river-colored water; the probable consequence of some streams falling into the bay, or into the ocean to the north of it, through the low land. Not considering the opening worthy of more attention, I continued our course to the North West being desirous to take advantage of the steady breeze and pleasant weather.

Later Vancouver learned of his omission from Captain Gray of the American trading vessel *Lady Washington,* whom he met on the coast some time afterward.

Onward sailed the two vessels to Juan de Fuca Strait, named after the oldtime Spanish explorer. The channel lies at the southern end of the island that is now named after Vancouver himself. Lieutenant Baker sighted a distinctive snow-crested mountain to the northeast, and according to Vancouver's pleasant custom of naming landmarks after his officers and friends the peak was named Mount Baker.

The ships were overhauled in the bay that Vancouver named Port Discovery. A camp was established ashore under Whidbey's command, a small brewery was built to replenish the ships' supplies of spruce beer—an antidote for scurvy—and Vancouver prepared to undertake a survey of the inland sea between the island and the mainland.

Most of the work had to be done in the small boats, for navigation in these uncharted waters was a dangerous business. In spite of all the precautions they took, first the *Discovery* and then the *Chatham* ran aground on submerged shoals. The next high tide lifted both ships off the rocks and neither suffered serious damage. Meanwhile, the local Indians were behaving in an unpredictable manner. Lieutenant Puget dealt with them by firing warning shots from his boat's little swivel gun above their heads.

The summer was now drawing to an end. The survey of Puget Sound, in the state of Washington, had been completed;

the ships had reached the northerly coast of the island. Vancouver decided he had done enough for the year. He had taken his ships through nearly 500 miles of dangerous channels and was nearing the coast of Alaska.

When Vancouver had sailed this gray and mountainous coast with Captain Cook in the *Resolution* in 1778, the latter had missed the opening of the strait between the mainland and the then unnamed Vancouver Island. Cook later sailed along the westerly coast of the island, still without realizing that it was an island. But by the time Vancouver had worked his ships northward into the clearer waters of Queen Charlotte's Sound, he knew the truth.

This revelation brought him no apparent mood of rejoicing. Vancouver gives the impression in his log that he found this coast of gray skies, blue-veiled mountains,

and constant rain a depressing region. Like Cook before him, he preferred the brighter, clearer skies of Hawaii; tall, frond-capped palm trees, bright sunshine, and friendly trade winds were more attractive than motionless, dark-green pine forests, low temperatures and chill winds. But what seemed to upset the highly efficient Vancouver more than anything else was the fact that days of cold, lashing rain frequently interrupted the work of the survey parties in the boats.

On August 28 both ships entered Nootka Sound. A Spanish pilot boat came hastening out to meet them. "The Spaniards aboard the vessel were ready to leap overboard for joy," Vancouver wrote, "for it seems we were so long expected that they had now given up all hope of seeing us this season."

The Spanish officer in command was Don

Juan Francisco Quadra. He was a bearded, dapper, and friendly old gentleman who insisted on showing the visitors generous hospitality. The day after their arrival Vancouver and his officers, who had been accustomed in recent months to eking out their ship's rations with berries, fish, and occasional roughly cooked venison, found themselves eating a five-course dinner off silver plates with solid silver cutlery.

An odd friendship began between affable and cultured Quadra and taciturn, matter-of-fact Vancouver. While the ships were being overhauled, they proceeded to haggle amiably over the minor points of the terms to be agreed on in order for Spain to give up her claim to Nootka Sound. At this time Vancouver gave the names Vancouver and Quadra to the large island they were staying on, but the name was shortened in later years to its present form, Vancouver Island. Quadra's name is still preserved in the vicinity. Opposite the mouth of Discovery Strait lies Quadra Island in the upper reaches of Georgia Strait.

While awaiting further orders from England, Vancouver sailed in October for the milder seas off California to carry on his survey. In November he dropped anchor in San Francisco Bay where "nothing was in sight except herds of cattle and sheep grazing on the hills." A few days later he was riding across the pleasant countryside to one of the lonely Spanish missions that were scattered throughout the area. The journey was a revelation to country-bred Vancouver. "The great beauties of this part of California," he wrote, "certainly exceed any in the known world. Few of our Noblemen's estates can equal the plain Woods and Lawns here to be met with."

The ships moved on down the coast to picturesque little Monterey, then the capital of Spanish California. There they spent two months and were joined by Quadra himself. The local Spaniards showed so much hospitality that when the ships were about to leave in January, 1793, three of the men deserted. Lieutenant Broughton also left the *Chatham*, Vancouver having decided to send him to England on a Spanish vessel with official dispatches. Lieu-

71

tenant Puget then took over the command of the *Chatham.*

Vancouver now made sail for Hawaii, where he wished to complete Cook's preliminary survey of the islands, land cattle given him by Quadra, and acquire fresh provisions. Although he refused to barter arms with the Hawaiian people, they felt such friendship for him that they were ready to accept less dangerous items of trade. Vancouver allowed no firearms to be carried ashore except pocket pistols, and they had to be kept properly concealed unless required for self-defense. Midshipmen were permitted ashore only with officers.

The sailors were given no shore leave at all. Vancouver's discipline was growing stricter with every month that passed. His health was beginning to trouble him, and this problem may have affected his temper, which was certainly becoming worse. His anger flared up badly over the suspected theft by some Hawaiians of certain trivial items aboard the *Discovery*. Menzies, the naturalist, wrote about the disturbance:

> Captain Vancouver . . . put himself in such a passion and threatened the Chiefs with such menacing threats that he terrified some of them out of the ship with great haste. The King in particular came running into my Cabin before I knew anything of the business, and instantly jumping into his canoe through the porthole, paddled to the shore and we saw no more of him.

The ships returned to Nootka Sound in May, 1794. The *Chatham* still wallowed and plunged clumsily, much to Vancouver's disgust, but under Lieutenant Puget's command she contrived to arrive a couple of days before the *Discovery*.

Vancouver hurried on northward. At the end of May both ships began the terribly

arduous task of charting the rugged, deeply indented coasts and innumerable fiords of British Columbia. Constant rain and wandering parties of semi-hostile Indians increased the discomfort of the men engaged in the survey work. Near Prince of Wales Island four or five canoes carrying some fifty or sixty Indians surrounded two of the boats, in one of which was Vancouver. The canoes closed to short range. Several warriors jumped to their feet and hurled spears that wounded two of the seamen.

No merciful discharge of weapons over the heads of the attackers served on this occasion. Vancouver himself gave the order to open fire. Eight or nine Indians were killed, and the canoes made off hastily to the nearest beach.

The survey went on all that summer of 1793. Drenching rain, hovering Indians, endless rowing for the men, eating and sleeping in cramped boats or in damp and draughty makeshift tents ashore were all part of the daily routine. But by September that year Vancouver's survey line had crept up to 56 degrees north latitude and ended at the headland he named Point Decision.

Battered by autumnal gales, both ships fled south to Nootka. No official dispatches had arrived yet from the English or Spanish government. Vancouver sailed on to San

Francisco and Monterey, but this year no friendly welcome awaited the tired seamen. The French Revolution was gathering force in Europe. The Spanish authorities in California were uncertain as to their country's attitude toward both England and France, and decided to receive Vancouver with chilly neutrality. Nor were supplies of fresh meat or milk or newly baked bread delivered to the ships by Spaniards. No din-

ner parties were held for the officers or entertainment provided for the crew. Even in the wine shops of Monterey the British sailors found that they were regarded with dark-faced suspicion.

Vancouver complained that notes from Governor Arrillaga of Monterey were written in "a sneering, forbidding and ungracious style." Puget referred sarcastically to "officers of a civilized nation with whom

England is now joined as a Friend and Ally." Arrillaga requested Vancouver not to visit any more Spanish ports in California, and Vancouver, glowering with rage, promptly ignored this request.

He was under orders to survey the coast southward to 30 degrees north latitude. Orders were meant to be carried out. Neither Arrillaga nor any other Spanish officials were going to stop him.

The ships went on down the coast to Santa Barbara near Los Alamos. They searched vainly for the *pueblo* of Los Angeles, or "the country town of the Angels," as Vancouver called it. Then, at the end of November, they reached the Spanish settlement of San Diego, met a more friendly Spanish welcome at that little port, and sailed on to Rosario, a tiny settlement in Lower California.

With the southern end of his survey now

complete, Vancouver again set sail for the Hawaiian Islands. He was having trouble with his crew by this time. Perhaps in comparison the Hawaiians now appeared as pleasant and less complicated people than surly seamen and semi-mutinous midshipmen. Vancouver wrote:

Our reception and entertainment by these people, who are generally referred to as savages, was so great that it would seldom be equaled by the most civilized nations of Europe, and made me no longer regret the inhospitality we had met at San Francisco and Monterey.

A British Naval store ship named the *Daedalus* was awaiting Vancouver at Kealakekua Bay. The vessel had sailed up to Hawaii from the convict colony of Port Jackson in Australia, and from her the *Discovery* and *Chatham* were able to draw urgently needed supplies.

79

When the *Daedalus* returned to Australia she took with her three midshipmen, Pitt (the son of an aristocratic English family) and Clarke from the *Discovery,* and Grant from the *Chatham,* whose conduct had decided Vancouver to get rid of them.

During his vessels' stay in Hawaii from January to the middle of March, 1794, Vancouver relaxed many of his harsh restrictions on the crew. He was delighted that the Hawaiians had cared for the Spanish cattle he had brought to the islands from California. The animals were increasing in numbers and were the forerunners of the herds in modern Hawaii.

King Kamehameha of Hawaii and Vancouver became friendly and entertained each other on a number of occasions. Vancouver, a shrewd politician, wanted the native ruler to place his country under the protection of Britain in order to pre-

vent the possible seizure of the group by some other power. Kamehameha welcomed this idea; the increasing number of white men in his little kingdom—some good, some bad—warned him that Hawaii's former independence would soon vanish forever. On February 25, 1794, Kamehameha, in council with the principal chiefs of the islands, assembled on board the *Discovery* and ceded the island of Hawaii to his Britannic majesty and acknowledged themselves subjects of Great Britain.

With a wisdom far in advance of that of the age in which he lived, Vancouver assured the chiefs that their native traditions and customs would not be abolished by England. He promised that the islands would be taken under a British protectorate and thereby made secure against exploitation.

But when Vancouver brought back to

England his news of this cession, statesmen greeted it with cool indifference. At that time Britain was at war with the French dictator, Napoleon Bonaparte, who had seized the mastery of almost all Europe. Preoccupied with this vast life-or-death struggle, which was destined to last until 1815, or another twenty years, England's politicians were in no mood to add fresh territories to the already vast British Empire. Yet until the 1820's, when American missionary influence, hostile toward Britain, began to become the strongest force in Hawaii, the Hawaiian Islands lay anxious and ready to become a part of the British Empire. They formed one of the few commercially worthwhile groups in the Pacific Ocean.

It was surely due to Vancouver's vision and intelligence that the Hawaiian Islands retained their independence throughout the nineteenth century. But Britain herself came out of the affair badly. The Hawaiian people, through Vancouver, had placed their trust in her. But by her own lethargy and indifference in the years that followed the Napoleonic Wars, Britain continued to disappoint those honest and unsophisticated people. And in the process she lost a splendid group of islands, which in later years she undoubtedly would have been eager to claim as her own.

Vancouver sailed back to Alaska with the determination to complete his survey during that coming summer of 1794. Much of the coast of Alaska still remained uncharted, but his health was worrying him. He knew that in another year's time he might be seriously ill.

In bitter storms and almost arctic temperatures—the temperature in Vancouver's cabin dropped to 7 degrees Fahrenheit on more than one occasion—the survey work began again. So great was the cold that the men in Whidbey's boats were given extra short coats made out of old blankets to wear beneath their wool-lined Fearnought naval jackets. They also wore heavy leather gloves, and two pairs of thick woolen socks under their thigh-length leather sea boots. Vancouver himself could undertake little boat work that year. He wrote:

> I set out in a boat early this morning, but was compelled to return to the ship at noon, being seized with a most violent nausea which developed into a severe bilious attack that confined me for several days to my quarters.

But the work went on. Skirmishing fights with Indians, intense cold, shortage of food, weariness and insufficient sleep—none of these afflictions could deter Whidbey and Lieutenant Johnstone or the splendid men with them in the boats.

The survey crept westward along, and in some cases above, the latitude of 60 degrees north. Cross Sound, Cape Fairweather, Cape Riou, Montague Island, and southwest into the gray, sullen waters of Cook Inlet. Then came a number of friendly visits to the stout-walled Russian trading posts on the western shore of that haven. Whidbey and his men were entertained with glasses of fiery vodka, thin black ci-

gars, and great dishes of strongly spiced venison. These visits made a cheerful ending to the great survey.

Across the sea beyond Cook Inlet, the long chain of the Aleutian Islands stretched southwestward into the foggy obscurity of a frozen horizon. Above the chain lay the Bering Sea. At its northern end, in a latitude of 68 degrees, lay the white frontiers of unnavigable polar ice.

Vancouver's expedition had proved finally to the world that the fabled Northwest Passage did not exist. In order to do so, his boats had covered a distance of ten thousand miles, most of it under oars. Returning in their boats to Baranof Island, off the coast of British Columbia, where Vancouver was awaiting them with the ships, Whidbey and his men had one last narrow escape.

The sailors were ashore, drying their wet clothes and cooking a meal, when Whidbey saw two large Indian canoes glide toward the shore some distance away. He ordered his men back into the boats. Hurriedly they pulled out to sea. They were barely in time. A large party of Indians burst out of the pine forest, near where the sailors had built their fire, and came running toward the beach brandishing spears and tomahawks. They had meant to ambush the sailors and attack them before the men had a chance to regain the boats.

The ships reached Nootka in September. There Vancouver heard with sorrow of Quadra's recent death. No official orders from England had arrived, so the final settlement of the international dispute could not be reached. In a mood of impatient resentment, Vancouver decided to wait for a few more weeks. "Thus you see, my good friend," he wrote in a letter, "I am once more entrapped in this infernal Ocean, and am totally at a loss to say when I shall be able to quit it."

By late October Vancouver decided he could wait no longer. The poor condition of his wooden-hulled ships made it essential that he sail farther south before the coming of brutal winter gales. At Monterey, they found that Arrillaga had departed and that a friendly Colonel Arguello was in command of the settlement. Through this officer Vancouver learned, to his great pleasure, that Spain and England had finally reached terms of complete agreement over the disposition of Nootka Sound.

In early 1794, Spain and England had signed an agreement entitled "A Convention for the Mutual Abandonment of Nootka." According to the terms of this pact, the land at Nootka, which had been occupied by the British traders until 1789, was to be handed over to an official representative of England. The English flag was then to be flown for a brief few hours, after which both Spanish and English representatives would withdraw their parties from the port. From then on, either nation could continue to use Nootka freely as a harbor, but neither Spain nor England was to occupy the place permanently or to regard it as their national territory.

This ceremony was actually performed in 1795, a certain Lieutenant Pierce of the marines acting as England's representative, and a Señor Alava as Spain's. Thereafter, Nootka Sound was deserted and disappeared from the pages of history. Typical of the leisurely ways of the British Government's Foreign Office, no one in that establishment had exerted himself to make sure that Vancouver was kept informed of everything concerning his North American mission that was going on in diplomatic circles.

At the end of November, 1794, Vancouver sailed for England. His ships reached Valparaiso in March, 1795, after a tedious voyage in which the *Chatham* continued to surprise everyone by her unexpected sailing qualities. After rounding

Cape Horn, both ships arrived in England in the autumn of 1795.

Vancouver's voyage lasted four years and six months, the longest known up to that time, and during it his ships covered a total distance of 65,000 miles. The *Discovery* lost six men through various accidents, but none through scurvy. The saucy little *Chatham* did not lose a single man.

Vancouver's own seafaring days were ended. Clearly his health was breaking down and he could never accept another command. His condition became much worse during the year following his return.

For some unknown reason, he did not reside in King's Lynn. He acquired a house in the pretty little English country village of Petersham near London, where he became busy with the writing of an official account of his voyage. Charles, his brother, helped him in this tremendous task.

Midshipman Pitt now reappeared. He had been sent home in disgrace from Australia. On meeting Vancouver in a London street, he angrily attacked him with a walking cane. Charles intervened and ended the squabble, but the incident caused much scandal and endless gossip, resulting in more damage to Vancouver's feeble health. Pitt's very unsatisfactory career in the Navy ended in 1802 when he narrowly escaped being charged with the murder of another officer. Two years later he was shot dead in a duel in England.

Vancouver calmly accepted the fact that he had not long to live. He worked strenuously at his writing, and in March, 1798, two and a half years after his return from the North Pacific, he had completed five and a half of the six planned volumes of his *Voyage of Discovery to the North Pacific Ocean and Round the World.*

"You will have to finish the task for me, Charles," he said to his brother. "Ask Puget to help with the rest of it. Make him my compliments, and tell him that if I hadn't been so set-about by this weakness of mine, I'd not have bothered him."

Two weeks later, on May 12, 1798, George Vancouver was dead. Charles and Puget finished the final volume.

* * *

Vancouver's achievements were greatly overshadowed at the time in England by those of the brilliant and world-famous Captain Cook. But American explorers, seamen, and geographers swiftly realized the enormous task he had accomplished and the astonishing accuracy of his charts. They paid many tributes to his work in 1819 when their country inherited all Spanish claims on the Pacific coast above latitude 42 degrees north—the modern boundary between California and Oregon.

Lieutenant Charles Wilkes, USN, who commanded a Naval exploration of the Pacific in the period of 1838 to 1842, declared that he constantly marveled at the accuracy of Vancouver's charts. During the famous Oregon boundary dispute of 1844, American politicians used Vancouver's *Voyage of Discovery* as the only reliable published work on that part of the

95

Pacific coast. A hundred years after Vancouver's death, his charts were, indeed, still preferred to all others by navigators in the Alaskan waters.

A later generation of British geographers and authorities on exploration gradually realized the injustice that had been done to Vancouver. One of them, Sir Percy Sykes, wrote:

> The Strait of Juan de Fuca, with its complicated system of channels and inlets, was surveyed with a thoroughness unequalled in voyages of discovery. Vancouver was finally able to report: 'I trust that the survey will remove any doubt and set aside every opinion of a North-West Passage.' Although he received little notice at the time, Vancouver's name is now honored as that of a great surveyor and a worthy successor of Captain Cook.